PURNELL LIBRARY OF KNOWLEDGE

Looking at Pictures

Published in 1970 by Purnell
© 1970 by B.P.C. Publishing Limited, London W.1.
Made and printed in Italy.
SBN 361 01539 9

Looking at Pictures

by Colin and Moira Maclean

Foreword by Sir Charles Wheeler,

Past President of the Royal Academy.

PURNELL

London

Foreword
by Sir Charles Wheeler

The authors' original treatment for children of a subject of increasing importance in the life of the new generation is very much to be welcomed. Young readers will get stimulus for their incipient awareness of art from the text and illustrations. The records of thoughts, feelings and circumstances of artists of all times from prehistoric to the present are simply told. Stories and legends of painters with descriptions of their methods and approach will fire the young imagination and promote emulation.

It is right, of course, that a book such as this should be very lavishly illustrated, and if the only good of *Looking at Pictures* were to encourage children to *look* at them then that were enough to justify its publication.

Because, in the years to come, leisure will increase along with technological advance, pursuits such as the appreciation and practice of painting are more than ever to be fostered. This book will help towards this desirable end.

Contents

Looking is not seeing

Ask any group of people to draw an object from memory, or a scene from imagination, and no two drawings will ever look exactly alike. For instance, look at the two pictures on the opposite page. Both are called "St. George and the Dragon" and both illustrate the same legend, but beyond that there is little resemblance. Why should this be? In the case of these two pictures, the striking differences are fairly easily explained. For one thing, the two artists worked at different times in history. Paolo Uccello, who painted the lower picture, was particularly excited by the new ideas about perspective in the fifteenth century. He experimented with the rules in order to make things seem near or far, but he did not use effects of light and colour that could have added to the impression of varying distances. As a result the figures look as though they are carved rather than painted. Also, art until this time had been mainly for decoration, in churches and in manuscript books, so Uccello's painting is decorative too.

Tintoretto lived in the sixteenth century, by which time the use of oil paint had been greatly refined. He was able to create all sorts of subtle effects with it. In his time the feeling was for drama rather than decoration, and so in Tintoretto's picture the princess seems to be rushing towards us, while weird light and sudden dark add to the atmosphere of tension and excitement. In fact, Tintoretto carried contrast so far, he was accused of treating art as a joke.

However, that is only part of the story. It is easy to accept that two artists *think* differently about the same subject, but surely we all *see* things in the same way? After all, we each have two windows in our head, through which we gaze out at the world. But it is not as simple as that. What, in fact, do our eyes see? The answer is, a jumble of tiny upside-

Right: Tintoretto (1518–94) **St. George and the Dragon**. *Below: Paolo Uccello (1397–1475)* **St. George and the Dragon**. *Both in the National Gallery, London.*

down images with a blank space in the middle. Of course, we know the world is not really like that, so our brain immediately corrects these faulty images; in other words, we see what we *know* is there. Babies do not have this knowledge, so their world must be quite different from ours. When someone who has been blind from birth is given sight by means of a surgical operation, he finds that, while he is able to look, he is not really able to see. The only things he can recognize easily are those he already knows well by touch. He has to learn to see the rest of the world.

If our eyes were just like a camera, the sizes of the objects we see would change constantly in a most alarming way. For instance, the image on our retina of a man ten feet away is twice that of a man twenty feet away. Imagine how odd it would be if a friend walking towards you seemed to double in size! This does not happen because we see people the size we know them to be. Look at your face in a mirror and it will look face-sized, but then let the mirror steam up and trace the outline of your image on it. You will find you have drawn something about the size of a large grapefruit. The image is very much smaller than you see it.

It is very important to understand all this before we start having a really good look at pictures. We should realize that there is no "right" or "wrong" way of seeing things. We all "know" about the world in a slightly different way, according to our education, our beliefs and even to the part of the world in which we live. For instance, a distorted room has been built by an American psychologist (who is also a painter) in which we see a man as a giant if he stands in one corner, and as a dwarf if he stands in another. Because we believe all rooms to be rectangular, we cannot see the distortion. On the other hand Zulus, who live in huts shaped like beehives and do not think all rooms are rectangular, are not deceived by it.

Renaissance artists worked out a system of perspective that they found to be the most "real" way

Structure of the human eye.

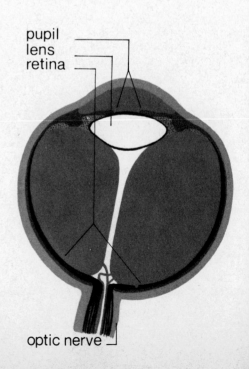

pupil
lens
retina

optic nerve

of representing things in depth on a flat surface. In fact, this technique is like a one-eyed, or camera's-eye, view of the world. For instance, in a perspective drawing of a tabletop, none of the angles is a right-angle. But whatever way we look at a tabletop, what we see is a right-angled tabletop. This is partly because we have binocular (two-eyed) vision and so see things from two slightly different angles at the same time, and partly because we *know* that a tabletop is a right-angled construction. However, we have become so used to things being presented to us in this way that we tend to think of pictures that do not use this system of perspective as "unnatural". This may apply to pictures dating from medieval times, to pictures from other civilizations, to pictures by untrained (naïf) painters or to the work of some modern artists.

In looking at pictures generally, it is therefore important to rid ourselves of all notions about what a picture "ought" to look like, and simply try to understand why any particular picture looks the way it does. To help in this, the following chapters contain information about the materials normally used in the making of pictures (called *media*) and also about the artists who made them – their ideas and beliefs, the times in which they lived and the kind of people they were.

Each time the distance between a figure (or object) and the retina is doubled, the image on the retina is halved in size. The brain corrects the image, so that we do not actually "see" people or things growing suddenly enormous as they advance, or tiny as they recede.

14

How pictures are made

ANY two pictures painted by the same artist will bear a strong resemblance to each other. This is because of the artist's own personal style – the visual language that he uses. But two pictures made by one artist, using different media, will look less alike than two in the same medium by the same artist. To understand why pictures look the way they do, therefore, it is important to know something about the methods and materials used by artists through the centuries.

Men have been making pictures for thousands and thousands of years, but only a tiny proportion of these have survived. Where they have, we can tell quite a lot about the techniques that were used. The portrait on this page is an Egypto-Roman painting; it was found attached to a mummy, in accordance with the age-old Egyptian funeral custom, but it is realistic and Roman in style. We can tell that it was painted by the *encaustic* method – that is, with colours mixed with melted wax, which were fused with hot irons to fix them.

One very permanent way of making pictures, popular in Early Christian and Byzantine times, was by the mosaic technique. This was simple, but very laborious. First small cubes called *tesserae* were cut from coloured stone, marble or glass. Then a full-sized drawing, called a cartoon, was drawn on to a wall and a small area covered with cement. The tesserae were then stuck into the cement. The most skilled artists in mosaic work always took care to see that the surface of a picture was not too flat and level, and there was a good reason for this. In early churches the windows were tiny and the interiors were lit by many lamps. The light of these was darkly and mysteriously reflected off the glittering, uneven surfaces of the mosaics. For the same reason, mosaics were made in very brilliant colours. The artists even managed to make gold and silver

An encaustic portrait of the 2nd century A.D. from the oasis of Faiyum, Lower Egypt.

tesserae by sandwiching metal foil between layers of clear glass.

About the thirteenth century artists started to use fresco, which was much cheaper than mosaic. The best way of making a fresco was by painting straight on to wet plaster. First of all, the artist made a cartoon, and this was rubbed on the back with chalk and the main lines were drawn over to transfer them to the wall. Alternatively, the lines were pricked and fine charcoal dust was "pounced" through them. If you look at the cartoon for Raphael's fresco, you will see that he used the latter method. Once the cartoon was transferred to the wall, an area sufficient for one day's work was covered with plaster and then painted with colours mixed with water. Because the plaster was still damp a chemical reaction took place, and the colours became fused with the wall itself. At the end of the day all the unpainted plaster would be cut away to be relaid next day. It is possible by counting

A 5th-century mosaic showing a procession of saints, from the church of San Apollinare Nuovo in Ravenna.

the number of joins in the plaster to tell roughly how many days it took to paint a fresco. This kind of painting is distinctive for its definite outlines and flat, chalky colours. It was carried out mainly by Italian artists, because the climate outside central Italy is not very suitable for the technique.

From the fifteenth century to the present day artists have most commonly used pigments mixed with oil. These are neither too fast nor too slow in drying, and they make it possible to blend one colour subtly into another and to lay down one glaze on top of another. Used properly, they are also permanent. Earth colours (umbers, siennas and ochres) are generally the most stable but some, mixed with oil, tend to become transparent as they age. For this reason you may sometimes see in old paintings figures that look like ghosts, with the background showing through them. Oil painting can be fast or slow, depending on the individual artist. Goya could paint a portrait in two hours, while Ingres is said to have spent twelve years, on and off, over one particular portrait. Pictures painted with oil colours have a rich luminosity and a variety of surface textures possible with no other medium.

The main disadvantage of painting with water colour is that it is difficult to correct mistakes –

Above: Albrecht Durer (1471–1528) **Country Dance** *(etching). Victoria and Albert Museum, London. Below: Thomas Bewick (1735–1828)* **The Chillingham Bull.**

Etching
To make prints by this method, a zinc or copper plate is first covered with a waxy mixture. The artist takes a needle and with this draws his picture into the wax. Then the plate is put into an acid solution, and the acid eats away (or etches) the lines that have been drawn. When the wax has been cleaned off the plate, ink is rubbed on to it and paper applied under pressure. A great many prints of one drawing can be made in this way.

although this does not apply so much to opaque water colour (gouache or poster colour). The advantages of this medium are a fresh, direct look and clear, glowing colours.

All these methods are for making single pictures. When an artist wants to make more than one copy of his pictures, he uses some method of printmaking. Basically, there are three of these; relief, in which the surface of the block is cut away till only the parts meant to print are left standing out (wood-cutting and wood-engraving); intaglio, in which the lines meant to print are cut or eaten away with acid, then filled with ink (engraving and etching); and planographic, in which a drawing is made on a flat surface (lithography). In the last method, the drawing is made in greasy crayon on stone or zinc, then the surface is damped and greasy ink applied. The ink is repelled by the damp areas, but sticks to the greasy ones.

In recent years, totally new media have been discovered. There are now synthetic (man-made) pigments, and these can be mixed with synthetic resins as well as with oil or water. The resulting paintings do not look quite like either traditional oil or water-colour paintings, but they have some of the qualities of each as well as new qualities that are entirely their own.

Raphael (1483–1520) **The Vision of the Knight**. *National Gallery, London. On the left is the cartoon and on the right the fresco. Note the pin-pricks on the cartoon. The completed picture is tiny —only seven inches square.*

Superstition and magic

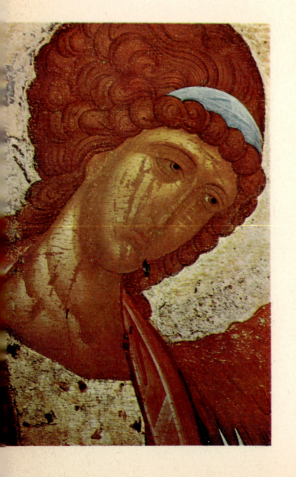

Andrei Rubliov school (15th century) **Head of St. Michael**. *Tretiakov Gallery, Moscow.*

ANOTHER reason for differences in pictures is that many artists have made pictures for magical or superstitious purposes. Pictures of this nature are as old as mankind itself, and yet some of them have come to light only fairly recently.

One day in the late 1800's a little girl was exploring a cave at Altamira in northern Spain along with her father, an anthropologist (a scientist who studies man). The cave had been found when a huntsman's dog chased a fox into it, and the anthropologist thought there might be fragments of prehistoric tools there. The little girl, who had run ahead, suddenly called out: "Look, Father! Bulls!"

And sure enough, there on the flattish ceiling were bison, reindeer, wolves and boars. Many people at first refused to believe that the paintings were thousands of years old. Where, they asked, would our primitive ancestors have found paints, brushes and even lights to work by? But we know now that they used natural earth pigments and charred wood, applied with reed brushes, and that they worked by the light of stone lamps. We also know that the paintings at Altamira date from more than a hundred centuries ago.

Two schoolboys and a dog were responsible for another exciting discovery at Lascaux in France in 1940. The dog had fallen into a hole and, following it, the boys found a cave full of wonderful paintings. The animals at Lascaux include deer, bulls, bison, a woolly rhinocerous and lions. Some are enormous – one bull alone is seventeen feet long. Brilliantly clear still, this work is covered with crystals formed over thousands upon thousands of years, so there can be no doubt of its great age. In fact, the paintings at Lascaux are even older than those at Altamira, dating from about forty thousand years ago.

These beautiful pictures give rise to many puzzling questions. Why were they painted? Why did such skilful painters make small and large animals look the same size? Why did they work on top of earlier paintings? The only satisfactory answer to all those questions is that the paintings had a magical purpose; our ancestors may have felt that possessing the image of an animal gave them power over the animal itself. The people did not live in these underground caves, so the spots where the paintings are were probably sacred.

One of the cave paintings at Lascaux. It shows a herd of horses and a much larger leaping cow, evidently painted at quite different times.

In paintings found in Ancient Egyptian tombs people are distorted to show head and legs in profile, but the eye in front view, and the shoulders are also in front view with both arms showing. This may have been to do with their belief that a dead person needed all his belongings, including his body, for use in his after-life. It was obviously important to the Egyptians to show as much as the figure as possible – never implying that any person had only one arm or leg, as could happen in a side view.

The rigid beliefs of the early Christians in Byzantium affected European art for many centuries afterwards. The head shown here is typical of the "frozen" Byzantine style. Figures were always shown in front view, and every face had a long, straight nose. No portraits of real people were ever painted – the religion banned imagery, and demanded symbols that stood for people.

Detail of an Egyptian papyrus, showing Osiris and offerings to the dead.

Pictures of people

Important people

OF ALL the subjects painted by artists, the human face is probably the one with the greatest fascination for us all. Most of the faces familiar to us in pictures belonged to people who were rich and powerful in their own time – not because artists found such people more interesting, but because they were the ones most able to pay for their time and talents. Kings, queens, princes and popes had their portraits painted time and time again, seeking visual proof of their own superiority. On the whole their Court Painters gave them what they wanted, but sometimes a clever painter gave a little more than had been bargained for. For instance, in Van Dyck's portrait of Charles I on horseback, the impression is not only of kingliness but also of a kind of sad, languid elegance.

The painting of the two ambassadors by Hans Holbein has a curious history. Holbein's English patron, Sir Thomas More, had fallen from power and the painter had to find influential new patrons as soon as possible. At the time Jean de Dintville, the French ambassador to England, was being visited by a friend, another young ambassador. Holbein painted a portrait of the two young men in such a way that people were sure to talk about it. For one thing, there is a very odd collection of objects on the table behind the ambassadors – a lute with a broken string, mathematical instruments, etc. There is also a very curious object in the foreground, which puzzled the members of the Tudor court enormously. If you hold this book in such a way that you are looking diagonally across the surface of the picture from its lower right-hand corner, you will be able to see that the object is, in fact, a skull.

One explanation of the contents of this picture

Above: Hans Holbein the Younger (1497–1543) **The Ambassadors**. *Opposite, left: Sir Antony van Dyck (1599–1641)* **Charles I on Horseback**. *Both in the National Gallery, London.*

is that they represent all the necessary equipment of a civilized man of the time. The broken lute string may symbolize the coming parting of the two friends, while the skull may be a pun on the painter's own name – "hollow bone". Whatever the true explanation, the picture achieved the artist's aim. By the end of the year, Holbein had joined the household of Henry VIII as Court Painter.

We are not sure who painted the portrait of Queen Elizabeth I in her wonderfully sumptuous dress. It may have been Nicholas Hilliard, who was the Queen's Limner, or it may have been an assistant painting in the same style. It is certainly painted in the way the Queen particularly approved – that is, without any shadows but all in "plaine lines" – and is as regal and impressive as any proud monarch could wish a portrait to be.

There were other, more practical, reasons for the painting of portraits: for example, painters often played an important part in the arrangement of royal marriages. Until trains came into being, a journey from one country to another was long, difficult and often dangerous. It was much easier for people thinking of marrying to exchange portraits than to arrange a meeting. For this reason, Henry VIII sent Holbein abroad to paint young women the king thought he might like to marry.

Below, right: artist unknown, but probably an associate of Nicholas Hilliard (16th century) **Elizabeth I**. *Tate Gallery, London.*

Above: Peter Paul Rubens (1577–1640) **Marie de' Medici**. *Prado, Madrid. Below: Titian (c. 1482–1576)* **Philip II of Spain**.

The picture of Cardinal Richelieu was also painted with a practical purpose in mind, as it was to be sent to the sculptor Bernini for the making of a portrait bust. Perhaps because of this, Champaigne has introduced no dramatic effects into the picture. He has concentrated instead on the fine, detailed modelling of the face and head, and the painting is oddly more impressive as a result. It is hard to look away from the cardinal's cool, impassive stare.

In strong contrast to this is Rubens' portrait of Marie de Medicis. As well as being a painter, Rubens was also a politician and ambassador and carried out many commissions for Marie de Medicis. He shows her to be a real monarch, richly-dressed and majestic, and also a woman complacent in the knowledge of her own wealth and power.

It is particularly interesting to compare the portraits of the two Spanish kings, neither of whom was a very pleasant character. The sombre colours and severity of treatment used by Titian in his portrait of Philip II truly reflect the sitter's nature, for Philip was an austere, joyless man and a religious fanatic. Centuries later, Francisco Goya painted Ferdinand VII with a savagery amounting almost to caricature. Looking at this portrait, it is hardly necessary to be told that Ferdinand was a harsh and cruel despot.

It is difficult to understand why Goya was tolerated as a Court Painter by the Spanish royal family at all, as he produced the most impudent portraits of royalty that have ever been painted. When the French novelist Gautier first saw the large group portrait Goya had painted of Charles IV and his family, he said: "A grocer's family who have won the big lottery prize". And that is indeed exactly what they look like. It is amazing that this painter, who showed kings as fat and greedy or savage and evil, princes as sly and spiteful and favoured ministers as nincompoops, should have gone unpunished. It was lucky for Goya that the royal family were too stupid to realize that their Court Painter was holding them up to the ridicule of the world.

Above: Francisco Goya (1746–1828) **Ferdinand VII of Spain** *(detail). Prado, Madrid.*
Below: Phillipe de Champaigne (1602–1674) **Cardinal Richelieu.** *National Gallery, London.*

Ordinary people

While artists have always painted the rich and famous in order to earn a living, they have also painted their friends and relatives just for the love of it. Sometimes the most interesting faces we see in paintings belonged, in life, to unknown and perhaps poor and unimportant people. It must have been quite a relief for an artist to paint people who did not expect to be flattered, or made to look grand and important. He would be able to paint his sitters "warts and all", without having to gloss over such defects as wrinkles, grey hairs, red noses and balding heads. Hogarth's portrait of six of his servants is a picture of this kind – quite obviously painted for his own satisfaction.

Hogarth was the first English painter to look at life as it was lived in his day and paint it with complete honesty. He was also the first English painter to make pictures really popular. Until his time only the wealthy had owned pictures, and even then they were almost entirely by foreign masters.

Hogarth first trained as an engraver, and then attended an art academy run by Sir James Thornhill, who trained his pupils by the simple method of giving them paintings to copy. Hogarth did not like copying. He had a habit of noting faces and expressions that interested him on his thumb-nail and later enlarging them on paper – a habit that must have added much to the life and sparkle of his work. However, Hogarth gained one thing from Thornhill, for he eloped with his daughter Jane. The couple had to marry without Jane's father's consent, for Thornhill was an important man, a knight and a Member of Parliament as well as a well-known painter, while Hogarth was just an unknown young artist. He did not even look impressive. Short in build and proud of it, he always wore his hat well tilted back to show off the scar on his forehead.

Fame and fortune were eventually to come Hogarth's way, mainly on account of the series of satirical, story-telling engravings and paintings he

Opposite: William Hogarth (1697–1764) **Heads of six of Hogarth's servants**. *Tate Gallery, London.*

made. These are the works for which he is still best known today, but his portraits deserve equal fame. He never made so great a reputation with these, because he was too truthful to be popular with polite society; few aristocrats had the courage to risk the blunt honesty of his brush. Most of the portraits Hogarth left behind, therefore, are of ordinary people – his friends and family, actors and actresses and servants. Despite his eventual success, and his acceptance even by people like Thornhill, Hogarth never lost his simple tastes and habits. On at least one occasion he even forgot that he

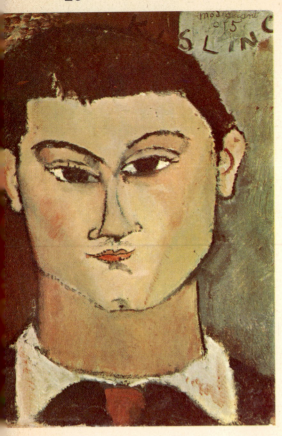

Amedeo Modigliani (1884–1920) **Portrait of Kisling.** *Private Collection, Milan. Based on negro sculpture, this artist's style is so mannered and distinctive that after seeing even one painting it is impossible to mistake his work.*

owned his own coach, which was waiting for him, and walked happily home in the pouring rain.

One of the very first pictures ever painted showing ordinary people in an ordinary room is the portrait of Giovanni Arnolfini and his bride by the Flemish artist, Jan van Eyck. The artist does not flatter the young couple or make them look impressive. Their faces are grave and tender, reflecting the solemnity of the occasion. The other unusual thing about this painting is that it is also a legal document. The artist was declaring that he had acted as a witness to the marriage – notice the signature in the centre, just above the mirror. It reads: "Jan van Eyck was here in 1434". The artist himself is reflected in the mirror. Arnolfini, because he is in the presence of God, is wearing his hat, but he has taken off his shoes because the place where he is standing is holy ground. The single candle burning in broad daylight is a symbol of singleness of purpose, and the little dog is a symbol of faithfulness.

There is a third reason for this painting being of special interest; it gives us a great deal of detailed information about the dress of ordinary, middle-class people of the time (Arnolfini was a merchant). Judging by the appearance of the young woman she may still have been following the fashion, current for some time, of shaving the front of the hairline and the eyebrows.

Jan van Eyck and his brother Hubert are famous for being the first painters to make effective use of oil paints. They probably did not invent the medium, but they achieved such remarkable results with it that it very soon became popular with other artists too.

Having looked at a marriage of the fifteenth century, now look at a married couple of the twentieth century. The painter, George Grosz, is being just as honest about his subject as is van Eyck, but what he is saying about it is something entirely different. The elderly couple in his portrait not only look weary and indifferent to one another, they also have an air of being corrupted by a life spent wholly in pursuit of material things. This biting, satirical art was first developed by Grosz in the form of cartoons, in which he attacked the German political regime.

Sometimes an artist's style is so strongly individual that it would seem to be impossible for the personality of his sitters to emerge at all. Amedeo Modigliani was such an artist. Looking at his paintings, it is instantly obvious that he was strongly influenced by the elongated, slit-eyed forms of African masks, as well as by the flowing lines of the Renaissance painter Botticelli. Nevertheless, a portrait such as that of his friend Kisling is still a painting of a very individual human being.

Below, left: George Grosz (1893–1959) **A Married Couple**. *Tate Gallery, London. Right: Jan van Eyck (c. 1390–1441)* **The Marriage of Jan Arnolfini**. *National Gallery, London.*

Groups of people

Hogarth's painting of his servants was not a group portrait, it was simply six portrait heads on one canvas. In a real group portrait the sitters are carefully arranged to make a satisfying composition. The painter should be able to tell us something of their relationship to one another by the placing of the figures, and by the clever use of the curve of an arm or the turn of a head. If you look at medieval pictures, however, you will see that artists then were much less subtle about this kind of thing; they simply made the important people bigger than the others.

In the family group by Frans Hals we can see the father, the grandmother, the mother, the children and a young woman who is probably a nursemaid for the baby. The father, placed centrally, is obviously the most important figure, and one feels that the grandmother is also a powerful influence in the family. The whole group has a happy, domestic air.

The lives of painters like Hals in Protestant Holland in the seventeenth century were very different from those of their fellow-artists in Catholic countries to the south. Southern artists received many commissions to paint vast canvases for the glorification of churches and princes, but the tastes of the devout, hard-working merchants of Holland were very different. Painters had to concentrate on subjects to which there was no religious objection, and the most important of these was portraiture. Many a worthy burgher, elected alderman, wanted a portrait painted to show off his new insignia of office, and local committees and governing boards wanted group portraits to hang in their meeting places. An artist who could please this public could hope for a steady income, but he could easily be ruined if he offended his conventionally-minded patrons.

Frans Hals painted nothing but portraits. All his work has a bold, lively quality and he himself seems

to have been a lively, jovial character, but he was always in trouble over money and constantly in debt to his baker and his shoemaker. As he had many children, this was hardly surprising. In his old age he was given an allowance by the Municipal Council of Haarlem, where he lived, and he painted his last two group portraits there in his eighty-fourth year.

Rembrandt van Rijn was only a generation younger than Hals, but he suffered even more from the drawbacks of working in Holland. At first very successful, he later offended his patrons and ended his life in bankruptcy and misery. The painting

Frans Hals (1580–1666) **Family Group**. *National Gallery, London. Hals was a jovial man with a very large family of his own. No less than seven of his sons became painters, and his wife was also a well-known artist.*

Rembrandt van Rijn (1606–69) **The Night Watch** *Rijksmuseum, Amsterdam.*

commonly known as "The Night Watch" was commissioned as a group portrait by a company of the militia, and shows Captain Banning Cocq (the central figure) giving his lieutenant the command to march out his men. It was later thought to show a night-watch going out on its rounds, hence its present title. However, the shadow of the captain's outstretched arm is thrown across the lieutenant's uniform and from its position it would seem that the sun is still quite high in the sky.

This magnificent group portrait made the militiamen furious. What they had wanted was a collection of clearly-recognizable likenesses, not people mysteriously emerging from shadows. Now thought to be amongst the finest works of one of the greatest painters who ever lived, "The Night Watch" helped to destroy Rembrandt's reputation as a painter and start the decline in his fortunes.

In America in the eighteenth century the situation was fairly similar. There were no princes or popes to hand out huge commissions to artists, and society consisted mainly of Protestant merchants who wanted portraits of themselves and their families. The group painted by John Singleton Copley, with its emphasis on solid respectability and family affection, was typical of American taste at the time.

However, we must not think that family portraits started even this recently. The medallion on this page, which shows a mother with her son and daughter, was made as early as the fourth century. The inscription, in Greek, reads "Bunerius the Potter", and is probably the artist's signature. What is really curious about this group is the familiarity of the faces – these people of sixteen hundred years ago look like a family we might easily meet in any Mediterranean country today.

Above: John Singleton Copley (1737–1815) **Family Group**. *Below: 4th century medallion in glass and gold leaf. Civic Museum, Brescia. The style of portraiture on this medallion looks rather like that on Egyptian mummy-cases of a slightly earlier period. It is possible that the artist was a native of Alexandria.*

Albrecht Durer. **Self-portrait** *(pen drawing).*
National Gallery, London.

Self-portraits

Artists have always used themselves as sitters — after all, what handier model could a painter have? Making a portrait of himself gives an artist total freedom to experiment with different ways of handling paint, and of representing facial characteristics. Self-portraits also provide us with a fascinating historical record, for they not only show us what an artist looked like, they also give us a strong indication of how he thought and felt about himself.

Some artists who developed their talents very young have even left us portraits of themselves as children. For instance, Albrecht Durer drew a beautiful self-portrait when he was only thirteen years old. Both Durer's father and his grandfather were goldsmiths, and the boy was intended to follow in their footsteps, but instead he insisted on being apprenticed to a local artist in Nuremberg. "My father was not pleased," he later noted. During his apprenticeship, Durer learned to paint altar-pieces and to make wood-engravings for the illustration of books. The latter had quite recently become an important craft, for the establishment of printing presses using movable type meant that books could be produced in large quantities for the very first time.

All his life Durer could sell his engravings more easily than his paintings in his native Germany; when he was short of ready cash, his wife even hawked them round local fairs and markets. But in Italy it was a different story. Durer's paintings made a great impression there, and he himself loved the freedom Italian painters enjoyed, for they were not tied to the old medieval guild system as were painters in Germany. On a visit to Venice he wrote to a friend: "How I shall shiver for the sun! Here I am a lord, at home a parasite." However, although he travelled widely, Durer always returned to Nuremberg. The self-portrait here, drawn at the age of twenty-two, shows a determined, ambitious but not quite self-confident young man.

Rembrandt also painted self-portraits throughout the course of his life, and we can trace his changing fortunes in these revealing pictures. The portrait here was painted in the last year of his life, and he has not spared himself. His features look battered by misfortune, and his eyes are weary and cynical. He has not even bothered to wear the odd, exotic garments in which he so often dressed himself and his sitters. These are a puzzling feature of many of Rembrandt's portraits, but they are in fact just a reflection of the artist's tastes. He had a large collection of strange costumes, and used them to add interest to his paintings. In this portrait, however, he seems too tired even to pose for himself; he is simply recording the fact that he is still alive.

Rembrandt van Rijn. **Self-portrait at Sixty-three**. *National Gallery, London.*

Children

Paintings of children are worth looking at separately because they set special problems for the artist and are at the same time of special interest. Royal children have been painted through the centuries just as have kings and queens, and for the same reasons. Posed stiffly in their grand clothes, they look at first glance like miniature adults. Jean Clouet's little prince, for example, is trying very hard to look grave and dignified. But somehow the fact that children are not impressed by their own superiority, together with their lack of patience for keeping still, lends a completely different air to their portraits. The tiny aristocrat in Goya's portrait looks just like a doll in his fanciful clothes, but the lurking cats with their restrained savagery make a frightening contrast to his innocence. Perhaps they are there as a reminder of the forces of power and corruption waiting to pounce on the little boy as he grows up, just as the cats are waiting to pounce on the innocent pet bird.

Looking at Velasquez's famous painting of the Infanta Doña Margarita and her young maids of honour, it is obvious that the little princess was unwilling to pose and gave quite a bit of trouble. One of her young ladies-in-waiting is trying to persuade her to stand still, and seems to be bribing her with something in a small red pot – perhaps chocolate. The princess looks wary, and gives the impression that she will take the first opportunity of escaping. It is said that one day Velasquez was painting the king, who was sitting in the spot from where we view the group, when the Infanta came in with her two attendants, her two dwarfs and her dog. Farther back a duenna and a courtier were talking, and beyond the open door another courtier was drawing a curtain. At the end of the room the king could see his queen and himself reflected in a mirror. He was very struck with the look of the whole group, and "The Maids of Honour", of which a detail is shown here, is the result.

Above: James Whistler (1834–1903) **Miss Alexander**. *Tate Gallery, London. Below: Diego Velasquez (1599–1660)* **Maids of Honour** *(detail). Prado, Madrid.*

It is hard to believe that the group held still long enough for Velasquez to paint them, and, in fact, the canvas is made up of separate pieces sewn together. But however it was done, it is one of the most beautiful and most revealing pictures ever painted, bringing the atmosphere of life in the Spanish court home to us with almost startling intensity.

Strangely enough, Velasquez's genius was forgotten for two hundred years after his death, until some of his admirers brought him once more to public notice. One of these admirers was James McNeill Whistler, who painted the lovely portrait of Cicely Alexander with its blend of Spanish realism and Japanese simplicity and sense of decoration. In a day when people stubbornly repeated that "Every picture tells a story" Whistler forced them to realize that a picture ought, in fact, to be a melody of line and a harmony of colour.

Born in America, as a child Whistler found all sorts of surprising things suddenly interesting to draw – like his own feet, when he was having a foot-bath to ward off a cold. He was a cadet for a time at the Military Academy at West Point (where he was known as "Curly" because of his unruly hair) but the only thing at which he proved talented was the drawing of caricatures. After a wild time as an art student in Paris he went to live in London, where he quarrelled with so many friends and made so many enemies that one feels he must have enjoyed doing it. He even wrote a book called *The Gentle Art of Making Enemies*. Like the butterfly he used as a signature, he flitted about the world and never stayed long in one place. The Scottish philosopher, Thomas Carlyle, was a neighbour of his in Chelsea and was having his portrait painted at the same time as Cicely Alexander. Carlyle grumbled about Whistler and the long frequent sittings he required and when, leaving the studio, he passed the little girl on her way in he would murmur "Puir lassie! Puir lassie!"

Many paintings of children, like the one of Gainsborough's two daughters, are portraits of

Above: Jean Clouet (d. 1540) **The Dauphin.** *Antwerp Museum. Below: Francisco Goya,* **Don Manuel Osorio de Zuñiga** *(detail). Metropolitan Museum, New York.*

members of the artist's own family. Gainsborough was born in Suffolk and spent his boyhood rambling about the countryside sketching the scenery. He must have had an exceptional gift for catching a likeness, for one day he sketched a man who was robbing an orchard and the man was later recognized from his drawing and arrested. He was not always on the side of the law, however, for another time he forged his father's handwriting in a letter to his schoolmaster, asking for a day's holiday. As he married at only nineteen, Gainsborough was a very young father to the two little girls in the painting.

In life Gainsborough's greatest rival was Sir Joshua Reynolds who painted "The Age of Innocence" – actually a portrait of Reynolds' grandniece, Theophila Gwatkin, aged six. Gainsborough's

Left: Sir Joshua Reynolds (1723–1792) **The Age of Innocence**. *Tate Gallery, London.*

Sir Joshua Reynolds
In his desire to achieve rich, deep colour Reynolds often used bitumen. This pigment gives very brilliant results at first, but it never dries. In time it trickles down the canvas, ruining its surface. Many of Reynolds's paintings are in very poor condition today, because of his fondness for bitumen.

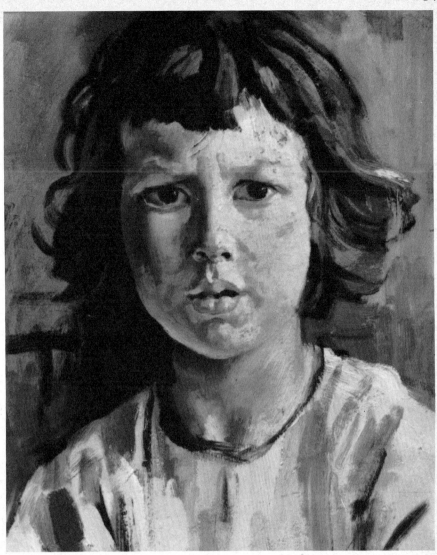

Above: Thomas Gainsborough (1727–88) **The Artist's Daughters**. *National Gallery, London. Right: Augustus John (1878–1961)* **Robin**. *Tate Gallery, London.*

aim was always to catch the charm and vivacity of his sitters, but Reynolds liked to capture qualities of mind or spirit. This is perhaps why Reynolds' six-year-old has a pathos almost too sentimental for our taste today, while Gainsborough's little girls still appeal in their fresh, flower-like charm.

Augustus John's painting is also a portrait of his own child, his third son. While other painters of his time were struggling to find new ways of expressing a world growing more complex day by day, John was an artist who simply painted in immediate, carefree response to anything that caught his eye. This quick, impetuous style was particularly appropriate for painting children, and he seems to have given us the whole nature of his young son in a few broad, dramatic brushstrokes.

People in pictures

People at work

IN THE last chapter we looked at portraits – in other words, pictures of particular people. But artists have always used the human figure in making pictures, quite apart from portrait-painting. This is because they have always been concerned with the subjects that are most familiar and important to all of us, and those subjects inevitably involve people. Here we have split them into three basic groups; people at work, play and war. As with any other subject, each artist has his own personal way of dealing with people at work.

Jan Vermeer was one of a group of seventeenth-century painters who were interested in recording the customs and manners of life in Holland. They painted little pictures of courtyards, the interiors of houses, tavern scenes, conversation groups and workaday life in general. This kind of painting is known as *genre* painting, from the French word meaning "manner" or "style", and Jan Vermeer was its greatest master. All his paintings have a quality of stillness and repose. Even when when he shows someone at work, as in "The Cook" there is no sense of hurry or strain, but only a calm, sunlit simplicity.

Although well thought of in his home town of Delft, Vermeer's work did not make him rich. When he died, he had nothing to leave his wife and eight children but twenty-six unsold pictures. Today these would be worth a very large fortune, especially as there are now less than forty Vermeers in existence. The scarcity of his work, plus the fact that he did not always sign it, has made Vermeer very popular with forgers. The most famous one, Van Meegeren, had painted and sold several highly-priced "Vermeers" before he was discovered and imprisoned.

The first artist to paint peasants at work in the

Jean Francois Millet (1914–75) **The Winnower** *(detail) Louvre, Paris.*

fields, not just as picturesque additions to a landscape but as real, toiling human beings, was Jean François Millet. Born into a peasant family, Millet had a hard struggle to break away from his background and become a painter. He achieved some success in Paris, but he did not really like having to live and work in the city. In 1849, a cholera epidemic drove him to move with his wife and babies to the village of Barbizon, where other painters had already settled. There he went on to paint scenes of the peasant life that he understood so well. Although these eventually made him famous, they also brought accusations that he was a dangerous socialist. While he loved to paint pictures in subdued colours, lit by a gentle evening light, Millet's main concern was to emphasize the essential dignity of labour. No artist before him ever expressed such a sympathetic understanding of farm labourers and their work.

Stanley Spencer was an artist with a completely

Below, left: Stanley Spencer (1891–1959) **Swan Upping**. *Tate Gallery, London. Right: Jan Vermeer (1632–75)* **The Cook**. *Rijksmuseum, Amsterdam.*

different outlook, who used scenes of the daily life in his native village of Cookham, on the Thames, to illustrate his own mystical ideas. His religious paintings are particularly unusual, for he peopled the Gospel stories with ordinary villagers in their clumsy, modern clothes. In his picture of the annual Swan Upping ceremony on the river Thames, the people at work – like the boats, the swans, the bridge and the ripples on the water – are used as vital shapes in forming the whole design of the picture. Of course, artists always take account of the shapes and patterns their figures make in relation to the complete picture, but Spencer took this farther than most. In his paintings, the shapes the figures make become more important than their qualities as human beings. As a result, his paintings have a flow and rhythm that is almost hypnotic.

Spencer painted with fanatical attention to detail, and planned his pictures with mathematical precision. Because he worked on very large canvases in a small room, he is said to have started painting at the top left-hand corner and then worked downwards, unrolling the canvas as he went along. This would be quite impossible to do unless the artist had already worked out a completely accurate "map" of the picture he wanted to paint, down to the very last detail.

Although the Industrial Revolution brought about huge changes in most people's working lives – changes that are still going on – there are some forms of work that have always remained basically the same. For instance, children still have to learn their lessons and teachers still have to teach them, just like the child and the young schoolmistress in Chardin's painting. Chardin was also a *genre* painter, but this time a French one. While Hogarth was painting his true-to-life pictures in England, Chardin was doing much the same thing on the other side of the Channel and, in the same way, making himself unpopular with the aristocracy. Unlike Hogarth, though, Chardin was never a satirist. He loved to paint quiet glimpses of ordinary people

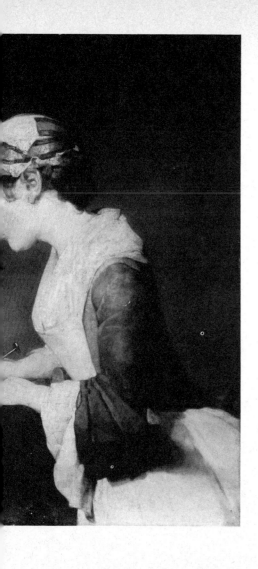

going about their daily tasks, without striving for striking effects or brilliant colour. There is a gentle, appealing charm about all his paintings.

Before he became Court Painter to Philip IV of Spain, Velasquez also painted simple pictures of a *genre* nature. Although he often gave these religious titles, their real subject was the work of ordinary people. Thus "Christ in the House of Martha and Mary" is really about a little kitchen maid and her work. We are very conscious of the girl's strong, work-worn hands and of the food and utensils on the table before her. The scene implied by the title is just a mirrored reflection in the background.

In a way both Velasquez and Vermeer painted the same subject, but how different in feeling the two pictures are! Velasquez's painting has an emotional intensity and a sense of dramatic happenings just off stage, but Vermeer has given us a peep backwards in time. It is as though he managed to stop the clock for a few moments one morning in 1658 and "bottle" the whole scene for us, sunlight and all.

Above: Jean Baptiste Chardin (1699–1779) **The Young Schoolmistress.** *Left: Diego Velasquez,* **Christ in the House of Martha and Mary.** *Both in the National Gallery, London.*

People at play

Pieter Brueghel was a Flemish painter who specialized in everyday scenes of country and village life.
He loved to show peasants going about their normal
business – working, hunting, feasting and cele-
brating country weddings. His paintings of people
at play are particularly enjoyable; there is nothing
rich or elegant about them, they just swarm with
hearty, boisterous life. Brueghel liked to get lots and
lots of people into his pictures – try counting the
figures in "Children's Games". But his paintings do
not look overcrowded, because of the high viewpoint
he used. We seem to be looking down on the playing
children as though from the upper storey of a house.

Because he painted peasant life so well, we might
jump to the conclusion that Brueghel himself was
born a peasant. But we would be quite wrong.
Brueghel observed rustic activity with a cool,
townsman's eye. It was fashionable in his day to
regard the country "yokel" as a sort of clown, and
to use him to illustrate the folly of the human race.

Pieter Brueghel (c. 1525–69)
Children's Games. *Kunst-
historisches Museum,
Vienna.*

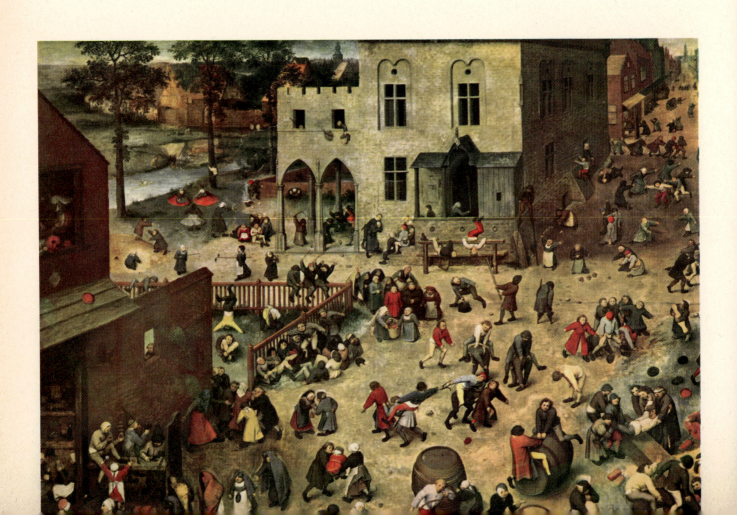

Georges Seurat

This artist worked in an unusually controlled and methodical way. While he was making sketches for **La Grande Jatte** *he even asked his friends to come along, bringing shears with them to cut the grass around the spot where he was painting. He wanted to make sure it had exactly the right kind of bristly, springy texture he wanted for the picture. The canvas for* **La Grande Jatte** *was so enormous that most of it had to be painted from the top of a step-ladder, so all this careful preparation of detail beforehand was very necessary.*

When Seurat's paintings were first shown in public, people laughed at them and called them "flea paintings" because of all the little dots.

Shakespeare used Quince the Carpenter and Bottom the Weaver in this way. Neither Brueghel nor Shakespeare despised peasants; it was just that country people made more honest examples of the types they wanted to show than townsfolk, who disguised their natures beneath a cloak of artificial "manners".

Brueghel's picture, as well as being complex and rich in colour, gives us a fascinating glimpse into the play of boys and girls long ago. Look closely at the children's activities, and you will see that their games are just the same as those played by boys and girls today.

Towards the end of the nineteenth century, French artists found most of their inspiration in people at play – enjoying themselves in cafés or music-halls or at the races, or just relaxing in the countryside. Georges Seurat was one of these artists. The Impressionist painters had already discovered the exciting effects to be gained by the use of pure, bright colours unmixed with browns or greys. Now Seurat took their theories one step

Georges Seurat (1859–1891) **Sunday Afternoon on La Grande Jatte**. *Art Institute, Chicago.*

further. He did not even blend his colour on the palette but applied it in dots directly on to canvas, leaving the final blending to the eye of the onlooker. This kind of painting is called *pointillisme*, and two examples of the brilliant, glowing results Seurat achieved with it can be seen here.

Seurat painted very slowly, and with tremendous care. For "Sunday Afternoon on the Isle of La Grande Jatte" he made twenty-seven drawings, and then about thirty preparatory oil sketches. As he worked so slowly, and as he died at the early age of thirty-two, he left only a handful of finished pictures. But despite his care and precision, he managed to create an atmosphere of relaxed ease and enjoyment seldom surpassed.

Like the games played by Brueghel's children, there are other pastimes that have been handed down to us over hundreds of years. For instance, the unsophisticated picture of an eighteenth century cricket match looks – apart from the clothes of the players and the shape of the bat – very much like a picture of any village cricket match today. But not all sports of the past that have been recorded by artists are still with us. Some have died out or been banned, like the cock-fighting shown in Hogarth's print. This was an exceedingly cruel sport, made even more so by the practice of sharpening the bird's beaks and attaching steel or silver spurs to their claws. Popular throughout the Middle Ages and for centuries afterwards, cockfighting also provided an outlet for the gambling passion of the 1700's. It was finally made illegal in 1849. Hogarth's picture makes it quite obvious that it was a very unpleasant sport. There is no air of relaxed enjoyment here, but only sly, greedy or snarling faces and a feeling of evil and corruption.

To return to something that has changed very little, look at the painting by Lorenzo Costa. Who could think, in the face of this, that the pop group is a recent invention? This trio from the Renaissance make it clear that it is, in fact, an age-old form of popular entertainment.

MANSELL

Lorenzo Costa (1460–1535) **A Concert**. *National Gallery, London.*

William Hogarth, **The Cockpit**.

W. R. Coates (?) (active mid-18th century) **The Cricket Match.** *Tate Gallery, London.*

People at war

Man's attitude to war has changed greatly over the centuries. For one thing, the value we place on human life is much higher today than it was in the past. Right through what we now call the Dark Ages, people had no importance as individuals. That is why few works of art made during this period were signed; it did not really matter who had created them. Only with the Renaissance in the fifteenth century did people regain their value as individuals.

Up to fairly recent times it was also accepted that life was a short and chancy affair. People died suddenly of mysterious illnesses and doctors could do nothing to save them. Families had many children, for it was recognized that only a proportion of them would survive to grow up. War, in these circumstances, was only one hazard amongst many.

As well as all this, war itself has changed. In the past, wars were comparatively small affairs. Weapons could kill only a few people at a time, not hundreds or thousands, and glory could be won on the battlefield. This meant that artists in the past could treat war as a colourful, exciting event. No recent artist, however, has seen it as other than horrifying.

In one of the most ghastly of all war pictures, Goya shows the shooting of a group of patriots who had resisted Napoleon's invasion of Madrid. The cool brutality of the soldiers' attitude and the terror of their victims make a nightmarish scene. Like many other Spaniards, Goya had hoped that the armies of Napoleon would carry the ideals of the French Revolution into his own backward country. "The Third of May, 1808" is a memorial to his shattered hopes.

Only a short time earlier, the grimly realistic scene called "Napoleon at Eylau" had been painted by Antoine Gros, who was a friend of Napoleon's and attached to his staff. Gros's war paintings were very popular with the general public in France,

Opposite, above: Antoine Jean Gros (1771–1835) **Napoleon at Eylau.** *Louvre, Paris, Gros's battle scenes were encouraged by Napoleon, who thought they were good propaganda. Opposite, below: Joseph Turner (1775–1851)* **The Battle of Trafalgar.** *Tate Gallery, London. Below: Francisco Goya,* **3rd of May 1808** *(detail). Prado, Madrid. Goya was the first artist to make an open attack on militarism.*

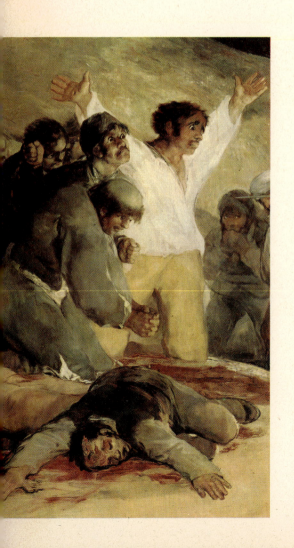

48

At foot of page: Paolo Uccello,
The Battle of San Romano.
National Gallery, London.

but they offended the followers of Classical art. Upset by their criticism, Gros gave up battle scenes and returned to scenes from Greek mythology, but he was never successful with these. Eventually, in a fit of despair, he drowned himself in three feet of water.

Many other artists were impressed by the horrors of the Napoleonic wars. Turner has captured for ever the supreme drama of the Battle of Trafalgar, with the great ships crowding in on one another, masts broken and tattered sails flapping, while billows of smoke from gunfire cloud the air. The wounded man at the base of the central mast is Nelson, dying at the moment of victory.

Turner was not a painter of war, like Gros. It was the splendour of light and its effect on landscape that interested him. Even as a young child, he was talented. His father, who kept a barber's shop in

Covent Garden, often displayed his son's drawings in the shop. Some of the customers were artists and they urged that the boy should be given a proper training, so at the age of eleven young Joseph went to take lessons in drawing. Later, he showed his work regularly at the Royal Academy, where he had a habit dreaded by the other painters. On Varnishing Day he would turn up armed with his paintbox, and would proceed to adjust the colour of his paintings so that their brilliance would not be dimmed by neighbouring works. However, he could sometimes be generous about this. On one occasion he darkened a landscape with lamp black because it was spoiling the effect of the paintings by Sir Thomas Lawrence on either side of it.

A fellow-artist, John Constable, once said of Turner's pictures that they were "airy visions, painted with tinted steam", and this description fits them perfectly. At the age of sixty-two Turner even went to the lengths of having himself bound to the mast of a ship in the teeth of a gale and a snow-storm, so that he could paint from actual knowledge of what these conditions felt like. He was always a highly-successful artist. On his death he left a fortune of £140,000, plus about three hundred oil paintings and nineteen thousand water colours and drawings.

The picture by Paolo Uccello was painted much earlier than the other war paintings here, and looks quite different – more like a chivalrous joust than a battle. This picture must have been very daring in its time, as it was the first secular picture painted in the Christian world. Uccello was also the first painter to attempt drastic foreshortening of the human figure. Look at the little knight lying on the ground. Of course, he is much too small, but other-wise he is quite successful – he does lie flat and he does recede. Uccello was not at all concerned about realism or accuracy in other ways. The horses in his pictures always look as though they belong on a merry-go-round at a fair, and the artist did not hesitate to paint them red if he felt like it.

The Bayeux Tapestry
This vast tapestry is stitched on linen and measures 231 feet long by 20 inches deep. In a series of 32 scenes, it tells the complete story of the Norman conquest of England in 1066. Starting with Harold's arrival at Bosham on his way to visit Normandy, it carries right through to the Battle of Hastings and the flight of the English afterwards.

On this page and the one opposite are drawings from one of the battle scenes.

Pictures of animals

An African elephant from a 17th-century book.

UNLIKE human beings, animals come in a wide range of shapes and sizes, and have many different ways of moving. They are clothed in a rich variety of textures and colours, and their natural savagery or timidity is not masked by any kind of affectation. All these things make them interesting to paint.

Some animals, like the elephant on this page, were painted for information, to show exactly what they looked like. Others, like the hare by Albrecht Durer, were painted for the artist's own satisfaction. Durer's picture is beautiful, but it is more than that; it also tells us something about the essentially wary, untamable character of a hare.

Both these paintings show animals in accurate realistic detail, but it is not necessary to do this in order to say something about an animal's nature.

George Stubbs (1724–1806) **Mares and Foals in a Landscape**. *Tate Gallery, London*.

Karel Appel (b. 1921) **The Cat**. *Tate Gallery, London.*

Karel Appel, a modern Dutch artist, has painted a cat that, at first glance, certainly does not resemble your own pet or the cat next door. You may say that it does not look like a cat at all, but you must remember that painters who want to emphasize some unseen quality have very often made their pictures rather unrealistic. Think of the Byzantine artists; they deliberately painted in a stylized way because they wanted to stress the spiritual, rather than the physical, aspects of the world.

Now look again at that cat, and you will see that there is nothing else it could possibly be except a cat. It is a painting of the *personality* of a cat.

Animals have often been painted as symbols of particular characteristics – for instance, a pig

Above: Albrecht Dürer. **Hare** *(watercolour). Albertina, Vienna. Below: Bull from a 12th-century bestiary. British Museum, London.*

might be painted to represent greed, or a sheep stupidity. In the Middle Ages there was a very popular kind of book called a bestiary, in which moral remarks were illustrated with animals used in this way. The animals in a bestiary were not very realistic, as you will see from the bull shown here, but they were interesting and decorative.

Another animal painted for what it represented was the little dog in Jan Van Eyck's picture of the betrothal ceremony. This little terrier was of a breed noted for its faithfulness, so the artist included it in his painting as a symbol of that quality. At the same time he managed to make it a tremendously attractive little animal, with its shaggy coat and bright, appealing gaze.

George Stubbs, who painted the picture of horses, admired animals for their beauty, grace and colour, and spent his whole life studying their anatomy. Of

Jan van Eyck. Dog (detail from the picture on page 27). National Gallery, London.

course, an understanding of bone and muscle structure is not enough on its own to make an artist great, but Stubbs was also a very talented painter. His studies simply enabled him to paint animals, especially horses, in a more exciting way. At the time of his death, Stubbs was writing a book on the comparative anatomy of man, tiger and fowl. It seems a very odd subject, but there is something even more curious about this book. Having been lost since the eighteenth century, the text and one hundred and twenty-five drawings turned up in 1957 in a Public Library in America.

People have often asked artists to paint, not only themselves and their families, but also their animals. Gainsborough's picture of the two white dogs is just such a painting. It is an animal portrait – a charming and truthful record of someone's favourite pet and its puppy.

Gainsborough and Reynolds

There are many stories told of the rivalry between Gainsborough and Reynolds. One of the most famous concerns a remark of Reynolds's that blues should never be massed together in a picture. Gainsborough promptly painted his famous **Blue Boy***, which was so brilliantly successful it put Reynolds very obviously in the wrong.*

Thomas Gainsborough, **White Dogs**. *National Gallery, London.*

Pictures of things

HOLLAND in the seventeenth century, newly freed from Spanish rule, enjoyed a great increase in trade and prosperity. The Dutch grew very aware of the material things that money could buy, and liked their artists to paint them. These pictures of things (known as still-life paintings) became enormously popular.

Painters used all sorts of tricks to make their groups of objects look as "real" as possible. One favourite was the dew-drop glistening on a flower-petal, and another was the half-peeled fruit with a curl of peel extending towards the onlooker. The two Ming bowls in Jan Treck's picture were of a type just imported into Holland from China for the very first time, and they must have aroused much curiosity. Treck emphasized their fragility by contrasting them with the solid heaviness of the pewter flagon.

Still-life has continued to interest artists. Paul Cezanne, who painted "The Blue Vase", was able to make a few simple objects look more solid and impressive than the elaborate arrangements of

Below, left: Paul Cezanne (1839–1906) **The Blue Vase**. *Louvre, Paris. Right: Jan Treck (c. 1606–52)* **Still-Life with a Pewter Flagon**. *National Gallery, London.*

almost any other painter. It was the weight and
density of things, rather than the effects of light on
their surfaces, that concerned him. Cezanne painted,
not to gain fame or fortune, but to learn as much as
he possibly could about the natural world. It is told
of him that, having finished a painting out of doors,
he would simply leave it under the nearest bush and
walk away.

Pierre Bonnard's vase of flowers is in complete
contrast to Cezanne's carefully-structured group.
Bonnard was a painter who aimed for glowing
colour and spontaneous effects. He grew more and
more free in style, and eventually made pictures
of pure colour, without any preliminary drawing. To
avoid doing anything that was a mere imitation of
nature, he even painted pictures from memory.

Pierre Bonnard (1867–1947) **Vase of Flowers**.

Pictures of places

The sea

FOR a long time it was thought that artists should paint only religious subjects or portraits, or pictures that told a story. Places were not thought to be a fit subject on their own, although they could form a background to a picture about something else. It was not until the 1600s that the painting of places came to be really appreciated, and even then artists usually felt obliged to introduce a figure or two, some ships or a few animals into their pictures.

The picture by Emil Nolde was painted in the twentieth century, and it shows only the sea. Nolde was a painter who used the subjects of his pictures to express his emotions. He painted in strong colours

Emil Nolde (1867–1956) **The Sea**. *Tate Gallery, London. The strong colour and vitality of primitive art appealed to Nolde, and he actually travelled to the South Pacific to study it in its own setting.*

with bold, almost savage, brush-strokes. In this picture he is using the sullen, threatening sky and the turbulent water to express a feeling of drama and foreboding.

The van de Veldes, father and son, painted ships and the sea. No one is very sure which of them painted what, as both were called Willem. In 1672 they were invited to England by King Charles II to draw pictures of sea battles (the ones his Majesty's ships did not lose!). There is a document still in existence, dated 1674, providing for an annual payment of £100 to the father for drawing sea fights, and to the son for colouring them. Most of their records of battles were painted from sketches made actually during the battles, from a small boat under fire in the thick of the action.

"Three Ships in a Gale", believed to be mostly the work of Willem the Younger, makes a pointed contrast between the fragility of man-made craft and

Willem van de Velde the Younger (1633–1707) **Three Ships in a Gale**. *National Gallery, London. Van de Velde's paintings of stormy seas made a great impression on Turner when he was a young man.*

the elemental fury of wind and wave.

By comparison the picture by the Japanese artist, Hokusai, looks at first glance patternlike and unrealistic. It is easy to overlook the two laden boats struggling in the trough beneath the towering wave, but, once seen, their impact is overwhelming. It seems astonishing that a picture so stylized and decorative should be so full of the feeling of the sea. Although Hokusai's print looks typically Japanese to us, his work was always more popular in Europe and America than in his own country. Japanese art followed classical traditions for many centuries, and Hokusai broke away from these. He was a strange artist, who spent years and years going from one master to another, experimenting with every branch of art and calling himself by many different names. He was always specially interested in illustrating novels, and it is likely that he himself wrote many of those he illustrated.

When Japan was forced to start trading with Europe and America in the middle of the nineteenth century, prints by Hokusai and other artists were used as paddings and wrappings for goods. There is a story that one of the French Impressionists, served with a piece of cheese wrapped in one of these prints, started the passion for everything Japanese that was to result in a completely different style of painting.

Hokusai (1760–1849) **Off Kanagwa: Hollow of a Wave**. *National Museum, Tokyo. Hokusai had a particular genius for enclosing the vastness of nature within the tiny areas of a woodcut.*

The countryside

Two of the greatest English artists, Turner and Constable, were born barely fourteen months apart. Both were landscape painters, but while Turner was always successful Constable could hardly earn his living. Turner's pictures, free in style as they were, had a splendour that fired the imagination. Constable's, on the other hand, were as peaceful as his native Suffolk – full of broken sunlight, shadow, and fleeting clouds in a wide sky. His art was, as he said "to be found under every hedge and in every lane". Looking for art in those places was a very daring thing to do in the early nineteenth century, and was not appreciated.

Constable developed slowly as a painter. He had barely started his studies when Turner was already well-known, and he did not sell a single picture to anyone except friends until he was thirty-eight. But although his work was never popular in England, it created a sensation in France.

One of the painters Constable particularly admired was Claude Gellée, the first really popular landscape painter. Rich Englishmen even had their estates redesigned to look like Claude's landscapes. We know little of this painter's life except that he was orphaned as a young child, was poor and

John Constable (1776–1837) **Salisbury Cathedral**. *Tate Gallery, London. Constable was fascinated by weather lore and meteorology. Many of his sketches have notes about the time of day and the weather scribbled on the back of them, in an attempt to pin down the effects of the fickle English climate.*

Samuel Palmer (1805–81) **The Bright Cloud**. *Tate Gallery, London. Palmer painted stillness, solitude and a sleeping countryside. This ink and wash drawing is full of interesting, leafy woolly textures.*

illiterate and may have been a pastrycook at one time. In spite of his wonderful skill in painting calm, airy landscapes, Claude hardly ever dared to leave out figures entirely. He used subjects from Classical mythology as an excuse for painting the scenery he loved.

The landscapes of some artists, like Samuel Palmer, are more dream-like than real. One evening, when he was a very little boy, Palmer's nurse showed him the moon casting the delicate shadows of branches on to a white-washed wall. He never forgot the experience, nor his love of moonlight. At only fourteen he had three pictures in the Royal Academy exhibition, but unfortunately this early success did not last. At one time he had to ration himself to one candle per night, and cut his living expenses to five and twopence a week. At his best he was a poetic painter, full of wonder at the moon and the small beauties of nature.

Strong light and brilliant colours attract many painters. Vincent Van Gogh, a Dutchman, went south to Arles in search of these. Described as a man "mad with colour", he transformed Nature into writhing, flame-like shapes. Van Gogh sold only one painting in his life, and that for a mere £4.

An enraged critic once nicknamed a group of French painters "Impressionists" after seeing a picture by Claude Monet called "Impression: Sunrise". The name stuck. Later, another critic referred to these painters as "five or six lunatics". Today it is hard for us to see what it was that infuriated people so much, but we must understand that in the nineteenth century paintings were

Claude Lorraine or Gellée (1600–82) **Cephalus and Procris Reunited by Diana**. *National Gallery, London. At the height of his fame Claude was already so plagued by forgeries of his work that he started to keep a "Liber Veritatis" (Book of Truth). In this he made careful drawings of all his paintings, as a safeguard against forgers. The book is now in in the British Museum in London.*

Claude Monet (1840–1926)
Poppies. *Monet's paintings are so gay in mood, it is hard to believe that for years he lived in dire poverty. His fellow-artist, Renoir, even had to steal bread from his mother's table to keep him from starving.*

expected to be "picturesque". When Monet painted a railway station, people thought it was an insult. In fact, what interested Monet was the marvellous effect of the light, streaming downwards through the glass roof to mingle with clouds of steam.

Light fascinated all the Impressionists. In order to catch its elusive, changeable qualities, they painted out of doors, directly from nature. Naturally this meant they had to work very fast, and people thought they were simply being careless and slap-dash. Now we are used to this way of painting and it does not offend us. It would be very hard to find Monet's delicate landscape with poppies shown here anything but a delight to the eye.

Vincent van Gogh
Van Gogh worked first in an art-dealer's shop but was fired for preaching passionate sermons to customers whose choice of picture he did not approve. Later he worked as a missionary among Belgian miners, who were alarmed by his wild, unkempt appearance. He won their trust at last, but by then it was too late. Disillusioned, he had already turned his passionate energy towards painting.

Vincent van Gogh (1853–90)
Cornfield and Cypresses.
Tate Gallery, London.

The town

The eighteenth century was an age of travel. Rich young men were in the habit of making a "grand tour" of the famous cities and beauty spots of the world, before settling down to a career. They liked to have as many souvenirs of their journeys as possible, but at that time, before the invention of the camera, they could not even buy picture post-cards of the places they had visited.

Venice was a city with many attractions for rich tourists, and several of its artists found it worth-while to devote themselves to recording its beauties for their benefit. One of the most famous of these artists was Antonio Canaletto, who started as a painter of theatrical scenery. When he turned to painting views of his native city there was a theatrical quality in his style that suited the splendour of Venice's palaces, bridges and canals very well. The demand for these views was enormous, and Canaletto eventually gave way to the tempta-tion to mass-produce them. He himself simply traced the outlines of each picture on to canvas, and they were then methodically filled in by his students. It was a great pity, for there have been few paintings of

Antonio Canaletto (1697–1768) **Campo SS Giovanni e Paolo**. *Art Gallery, Dresden.*

city scenes to compare with his earlier works.

Another artist who specialized in towns was Jan van der Heyden, who painted the view of Cologne shown here. The Dutch thought of painters as craftsmen like carpenters or plumbers, and expected them to do a good, sound, everyday job, with no flights of fancy. Once there were enough painters to form a guild of their own they were no longer forced to join the wooden-shoemakers' guild, but they still had a hard time earning their bread and butter. Van der Heyden was one of the few who got around this, for he invented a fire-engine and made quite a lot of money out of it. He also took an interest in the improvement of street-lighting, and was altogether very involved in town life. His strong feeling for it shows clearly in his paintings.

Although the Industrial Revolution brought a new kind of squalor and misery into life in large towns and cities, there were always painters who

Jan van der Heyden (1637–1712) **View of Cologne**. *National Gallery, London.*

Whistler
*All Whistler's paintings
show his love for simplicity
and harmony. He even
carried this into his private
life, by painting his walls
in plain colours or white,
instead of using the
heavily-patterned wall-
papers popular at the time.
He was a good cook, but
his guests had to be pre-
pared to face pale green
butter, or a pudding tinted
to match the walls of the
room.*

could look beneath these and find beauty. Whistler was just such a painter. He loved the Thames Embankment with its wharfs, warehouses, barges and bridges. He once forced guests who had come for supper to stay all night, so that he could take them to the Embankment at dawn and show them the sunrise. He also loved to wander there at dusk, when other people were hurrying home to shut themselves cosily indoors and draw the blinds.

The art critic, John Ruskin, once accused Whistler of asking two hundred guineas "for flinging a pot of paint in the public's face". "Old Battersea Bridge" was one of the paintings to which he referred. Whistler sued Ruskin for libel, but though he won the case he was awarded only a farthing in damages.

*James Whistler, **Old Battersea Bridge**. Tate Gallery,
London.*

Naïf pictures

NOT everyone who likes to paint pictures has been taught how to do it; thousands and thousands of people paint as a hobby. Very occasionally, we find an amateur painter whose very ignorance of what "ought" to be done seems to help him, or her, to express a fresh, child-like wonder at the world. We call painters like this naïf, meaning that they are simple and unaffected. A naïf artist paints all the objects in a picture separately, with no attempt to relate them to each other or to apply the rules of perspective. He usually uses strong, clear colours and may well paint every single leaf on a tree, or every blade of grass on a lawn.

Naïf painters have always existed, but until the nineteenth century no one paid any attention to them – partly because no one ever saw their pictures except personal friends. Then, in 1884, the *Salons des Artists Independants* was opened in Paris. Anyone who wanted to could hang his paintings in this exhibition. A former customs officer called Henri Rousseau, who lived in the suburbs, trundled his pictures across Paris in a wheel-barrow to it, year after year. Soon he was noticed by professional artists. They were very surprised to realize that Rousseau had, by instinct, stumbled on a way of doing exactly those things in which they themselves were interested.

Almost all young children are naïf artists, and can make very exciting pictures. This is because they are content to paint things just as they think they are, without worrying about whether or not they are "right" by anyone else's standards. Many modern artists value their untrained simplicity and freedom of imagination. It is a very exceptional person who can carry this imaginative quality on unspoiled into adult life, and a really great artist who can not only keep it, but use all his training and skill to enrich it.

Rousseau
Known as "Le Douanier" because of his work as a customs-officer, Rousseau was entirely self-taught. He claimed that his jungle scenes were memories of army service in Mexico, but it is now known that in fact he was never there. His exotic fantasies were based entirely on long hours spent in the Paris botanic gardens and zoo.

Henri Rousseau (1844–1910)
The Snake Charmer.
Louvre, Paris.

*Drawing by a seven-year-old
school-child.*

Pictures of ideas

WE HAVE seen how artists concerned with things of the mind have usually painted in a rather unrealistic way, compared with those interested in physical appearances. Sooner or later, someone was bound to take this one step further. For about seventy years now, some artists have painted pictures that are really ideas in visible form. They often start with the kind of familiar things that artists have painted for centuries, and go on to simplify these and rearrange their structural parts. What they finally show us is an idea about these things, rather than exactly what they are. In fact they abstract, or take out, their essential character and remove it from their visual appearance. That is why we call this type of painting abstract art.

William Scott is an artist of this kind. "Ochre Painting" is based on objects on a tabletop, which

Victor Vasarely (b. 1908) **Nives II**. *Tate Gallery, London. Vasarely has always thought that art in the 20th century should be "very close to science", but also acceptable as a part of normal, everyday life.*

William Scott (b. 1913) **Ochre Painting**. *Tate Gallery, London.*

rises so steeply that the picture looks rather like a landscape with a high horizon. In a way, this is just what it is – a landscape, but one that can be explored only in the mind.

Some modern artists try to give shape to things that do exist outside the mind, but have no outline or tangible form – things like light, sound and movement. One way of doing this is to use the way the human eye works, and play deliberate tricks on it. It is possible to paint shapes that seem to be sometimes behind, and sometimes in front of, one another. When we stare at a painting like this for several minutes, the whole thing seems to move. The artist achieves this by clever arrangement, and by the colours he uses. Some colours, for instance, are known to "advance" or "recede", and others seem to shimmer when placed side by side. All these tricks can produce an effect of movement, rhythm or changing light. Victor Vasarely's painting "Nives II" is just such an exploration of visual effects.

Pictures that tell a story

Religion

PICTURE story-telling is the oldest kind of story-telling there is. During the Middle Ages, when most people could not read, it was also the most important kind. At that time the Church ruled art, and the only stories that could be told were those from the Bible or the lives of the saints. But there were no walls in the churches on which to paint or hang pictures. They were built in the style we now call Gothic with tall, narrow pillars set very close together, and what space there was between the pillars had to be used for windows. There was only one answer to the problem, and it can still be seen in the brilliant, glowing picture-windows of Gothic cathedrals.

Towards the end of this period came the Age of Chivalry, and the picture by Gentile da Fabriano belongs to this time of colourful pageantry and courtly elegance. It tells its story clearly, with the simple imagery of a child's dream.

Vittorio Carpaccio, who painted "St. Jerome and the Lion", specialized in story-telling. He usually painted several large pictures of each story, like a

Detail of a stained glass window from Sens Cathedral. It dates from the early 13th century and shows the seizing of Christ.

Vittore Carpaccio (c. 1465–1526?) **The Brothers Fleeing from St. Jerome's Lion** *(detail). Venetian Galleries. Notice the animals in the background. Unlikely or exotic creatures like these were very popular with the Venetians.*

Gentile da Fabriano (c. 1370–1427) An episode from the **Histories of St. Nicholas**. *Vatican, Rome.*

set of scenes from a play. These pictures by Italian artists were generally commissioned by rich patrons, who would then donate them to the Church. Anxious that no one should forget their generosity, the patrons would often ask to be included in the pictures. Standing around looking interested, or perhaps heavily disguised as a king or a wise man, they intrude into many a biblical scene.

The greatest genius of the Renaissance, Leonardo da Vinci, also painted religious scenes. Leonardo was an extraordinary man – artist, engineer, composer and scientist. As if this were not enough, he was handsome, charming and exceptionally strong. He was so good at so many things, it was hard for him to finish anything he started to do. No sooner would he have begun some magnificent painting or piece of sculpture, than he would get a tremendous idea about designing a submarine or building a new kind of gun. He left behind many notebooks full of his thoughts and drawings, but the writing goes from right to left and must be held in front of a mirror to be read. Being left-handed, Leonardo probably found it easy to write like this, but he may have had other reasons for doing it, too. Even at a time when many new ideas

*Rembrandt van Rijn, **Belshazzar's Feast**. National Gallery, London. Paintings like this gave Rembrandt a marvellous chance to indulge his taste for splendid and elaborate costume.*

were in the air his theories were dangerously advanced; one entry that reads simply "The sun does not move" would have caused an outcry in the early 1500's.

In painting "The Madonna of the Rocks" Leonardo presented the holy family in a very strange way. No one knows why he placed them in that weird, sunless grotto, among gloomy rocks and colourless plants. His skill in realism was unsurpassed, but here he carried it so far that the faces look waxen in their perfection.

In spite of the Dutch dislike of religious art, Rembrandt also painted biblical stories. His enormous, dramatic "Belshazzar's Feast" may have been painted for Jewish friends, for the writing on the wall is in the correct Hebrew characters and is written in the correct way, going downwards from the upper right-hand corner.

Leonardo

Despite his genius, Leonardo was not a quick worker. While a guest of the Duke of Milan, he was painting his famous **Last Supper** *for a nearby priory. The Prior asked the Duke to speak sharply to Leonardo about "mooning about" instead of getting on with his work. Leonardo explained to the Duke that there were two heads still to be painted. He felt, he said unable to express either the celestial beauty of Jesus or the evil of the man who had betrayed him. But to save time, he added, he would look no further for Judas but simply give him the head of the prior.*

The Duke laughed, and told the Prior to let Leonardo finish his work in peace.

Leonardo da Vinci (1452–1519) **The Madonna of the Rocks**. *National Gallery, London. This strange but superbly-drawn scene shows Mary bringing the infant St. John to be blessed by the Christ Child.*

Myths and fantasy

As the pressure to produce purely religious pictures lessened, artists were able to give a much freer rein to their imagination. Some chose to re-interpret ancient myths and legends, while others preferred to create fantasies of their own.

Unlike their Dutch neighbours, Flemish artists seemed to be free to paint religious or secular subjects, just as they pleased. Most of them were interested in portraiture, but Hieronymus Bosch was an exception. For him, men and women had little dignity or individuality, but served only to symbolize the folly of the whole human race. Although the great thinkers of the Renaissance were gradually spreading enlightenment throughout Europe, northern countries like Flanders remained medieval in outlook for quite a long time. Necromancy (communication with the dead) was a popular passion, and so were alchemy (trying to turn base metals into gold) and astrology (reading the stars). Notions from all these "magical" sciences appear in Bosch's paintings, which makes it very hard for us to understand them today.

Bosch was also concerned with exposing the evils of the monks and other clergy. Although he died the year before Martin Luther condemned the practices of the Church, the nightmarish scenes he painted foreshadowed the dark days of the Reformation soon to come.

At exactly the same time as Bosch was painting his visions of damnation in Flanders, an artist called Sandro Botticelli was lending his distinctive charm to religious and mythological stories in Florence. The attitude of the people of Florence to their artists, in the fifteenth century, was rather like our own attitude to pop stars, television personalities and sporting heroes today. Everyone knew of them and told stories about them, and they were often given popular nicknames by which we still know them. Paolo Uccello, for example, means "Paul the Bird", because this artist was interested

Above: Sandro Botticelli (c. 1445–1510) **The Birth of Venus**. *Uffizi, Florence. Opposite page: Hieronymus Bosch (c. 1450–1516) Detail from the centre panel of the triptych* **The Garden of Earthly Delights**. *Prado, Madrid. Below: Sandro Botticelli, the Three Graces, from* **Primavera**. *Uffizi, Florence.*

in birds. Another famous painter, who was notorious for never paying his bills, became Tommaso Masaccio, or "Troublesome Tom". In the same way, Botticelli was born Alessandro Filipepo. The name by which we know him actually means "Little Barrel".

It is for his paintings of mythological stories that we know Botticelli best today. He made more use of flowing line than any other painter, and there is a wistful quality about his decorative nymphs and goddesses.

A later Italian artist, Piranesi, made etchings of fantasies based on architecture. Although these do not look like Bosch's paintings, they have a similar, nightmarish feeling of twisted reality. One particular series of etchings shows vast,

labyrinthine imaginary prisons in which the tiny figures of the prisoners are completely dominated by the menacing structures around them. Piranesi's work had quite a noticeable effect on architecture and theatre design in the eighteenth century.

An artist who might be considered a modern counterpart of Bosch and Piranesi is René Magritte, who painted "Time Transfixed". Here again we see real things painted in a very realistic way, but given a twist that makes them somehow alarming. Everyday objects are seen to have a threatening quality that no imaginary creature from outer space could ever equal. Painters who work in this way are now called Surrealists. The fantasies they paint are very similar to those our minds create when we are asleep and dreaming.

Not all pictures that tell the story of a painter's

Giambattista Piranesi (1720–1778) One of a series of etchings called **Carceri d'Invenzione** *(Imaginary Prisons).*

René Magritte (b. 1898) **Time Transfixed**. *Tate Gallery, London. Like Bosch, Magritte introduces us to a world made strange by commonplace objects that are too large, too small or in the wrong place. What he is telling us is not easy to explain, because it probably means something quite different to each person who looks at his paintings.*

own private dream-world are menacing. Marc Chagall is a painter of poetic fantasies, many of which are happy in mood and full of lively charm. Born in a Russian village, Chagall, like many painters from different parts of the world, came to Paris in the early years of this century. He felt very homesick for his native village, and painted many pictures of his memories of it. In these imaginative scenes, people and things can be any colour at all, houses are built upside-down, cows can fly and fish can play the fiddle. Chagall painted only one picture of Paris during his first stay there, and it tells the story of his restless unease in the city. It is impossible for us to guess the exact meaning of the fallen figures,

Paul Klee (1879–1940) **The Twittering Machine**. *Museum of Modern Art, New York.*

the upside-down train, the cat with the human face and the parachutist descending from the sky, but we can see that they are symbols of distress. Shortly after painting this picture Chagall went back to Russia, and after the Revolution he was put in charge of fine arts in his area. However, he was quite incapable of turning out earnest pictures of dutiful workers, or stern portraits of Marx and Lenin. He had an irrepressible tendency to paint fish with umbrellas and cows jumping over the moon. The authorities disapproved, so he had to go back to France.

Whereas Chagall's fantasies are poetic, those of another modern painter, Paul Klee, are full of wit and irony. The images in Klee's pictures are simple and almost child-like. He wanted to be able to see with completely fresh, unprejudiced vision, as though he were newly-born and knew nothing about the world or about art. His pictures are mostly tiny, and drawn with a thin, wiry, slightly blotchy

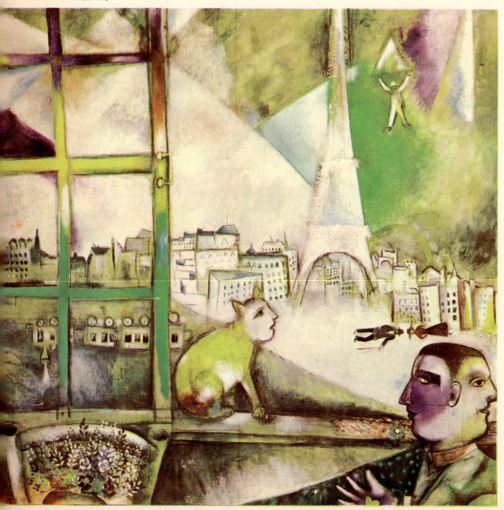

Marc Chagall (b. 1887) **Paris Through the Window**. *Solomon R. Guggenheim Foundation, New York. Although the title of this picture implies that it is a view of Paris, it is really the story of the kind of life the artist lived in that city.*

line. They are both funny and mysterious, even if we know little or nothing about the conditions in pre-war Europe that inspired them. If we do know something about those conditions, Klee's humour takes on a deeper and more ironic meaning.

It is easy to say that, since the development of photography, artists have been deprived of their traditional job of recording physical appearances, and so have had to turn to abstraction or fantasy. There is a grain of truth in this, but it is not the whole story. There were no cameras in the days of Bosch and Piranesi, for instance. The creation of a fantasy world has always provided the artist with an indirect means of making dangerous political and social comment. It has also been a way of expressing his own personal hopes and fears about the state of the world. It may be that the increasing pressures and threats of our complex modern society are leading more and more artists to turn to fantasy, as a way of giving vent to their feelings.

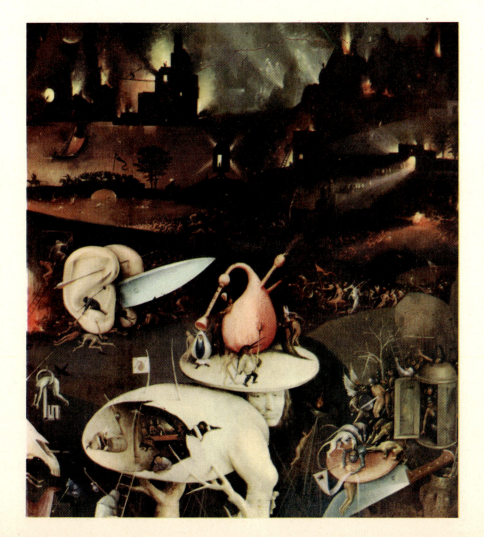

*Hieronymus Bosch. Right wing of the triptych **The Garden of Earthly Delights** (detail). Prado, Madrid. There is no doubt that the strange creatures and incident's in Bosch's paintings had an exact meaning for people in his own time, but even by the sixteenth century their significance had been lost. Today we can only appreciate his pictures for their weirdly imaginative atmosphere and for the jewel-like quality of the painting.*

Real life

William Hogarth was an artist who liked to paint a series of pictures telling the same story, and he actually invented the stories he told. He did not do this because he wanted to create imaginary places or people – far from it! A fiery little cockney, Hogarth despised the eighteenth century passion for everything foreign. He wanted an English art for the English people, and was determined to give it to them even if he had to force it down their throats. He made up his stories in order to show up all that was corrupt and foolish about life in the London of his day.

"The Rake's Progress" is probably the best known series of Hogarth's story-telling pictures. It shows

William Hogarth, **The Mad-house** *from* **The Rake's Progress**. *Sir John Soane's Museum, London. Hogarth liked to think of his paintings as a stage, and the figures in them as actors and actresses miming his story.*

MANSELL

the gradual downfall of a wealthy, fashionable young man (the "rake") through taking up with bad company and living beyond his means. Hogarth used the last episode in the story to expose the appalling conditions suffered by the insane in the wretched asylums of the time. The rake, the grinning fiddler, the foolish singer, the blind man with his paper telescope and the others all share the same dark, squalid cell.

Hogarth made his pictures popular by making engravings of them, which he sold cheaply. For the first time, people other than the rich could hang pictures on their walls. The great demand for these engravings led other people to copy them. Because of this, Hogarth managed to get Parliament to pass a Copyright Act, protecting all artists and engravers against forgeries of their work.

While few artists have told stories at such length as Hogarth did, there are many who have told us a great deal about what it was like to live in a particular place at a particular time. These are not painters of landscape for its own sake, like Turner,

Laurence Stephen Lowry (b. 1887) **Coming out of School**. *Tate Gallery, London. Lowry has spent his whole life creating a totally personal kind of art out of the life lived in the back streets of industrial Manchester.*

Constable or Claude. They have something definite to say about what life is like in the places they paint, and for this reason they are included here among the painters who have a story to tell.

L. S. Lowry is an artist who has spent his life in the industrial north of England. His theme is how man lives in the environment he has created for himself, rather than the one Nature gave him. All his paintings show mean streets with smoke-blackened houses, huddling in the lee of great warehouses and factories with belching chimneys. Stick-like people scurry around like ants but, looked at closely, they separate into individuals – the lonely, dejected ones, the brisk, bustling ones, and the resigned, plodding ones.

Hendrik Avercamp painted life in seventeenth century Holland in much the same way. His pictures are more detailed than Lowry's, and the lives of the tiny people in them much more dominated by Nature. Avercamp particularly loved the effects of winter. We can pick out the individuals in his crowds, for they are very vivid and expressive of gesture – perhaps because Avercamp himself was born dumb.

Gustave Courbet (1819–1877) **Funeral at Ornans**. *Louvre, Paris. Courbet was not an imaginative artist; he would only paint what he could see and touch. Once a patron asked him for a picture with angels in it. "Angels!" exclaimed Courbet, "but I have never seen angels. What I have not seen I cannot paint."*

The mid-nineteenth century was a bad time for an artist like Gustave Courbet, who wanted to paint only true stories from real life. At that time, people liked to overlook the blunter facts of life, and they were easily shocked. Women were supposed to be pure, fragile creatures with no legs, and even pianos had their legs decently frilled. Children were supposed to be little angels, who enjoyed the endless sermons that were read to them. It was a world of false piety and pretence, and Courbet would not have any part of it. Pictures like his "Funeral at Ornans" which tells the true story of the burial of his own grandfather, were not very popular.

Hendrik Avercamp (1585–1634) **Skaters near a Castle**. *National Gallery, London.*

Pictures in books

SINCE we have been looking at pictures that tell a story without any words, it is interesting to go on to look at pictures that illustrate the words of a story. The first "real" printed books as we know them were illustrated with wood-engravings. By the middle of the sixteenth century, however, people wanted to see really detailed drawings of the things described in a book, or life-like portraits of the characters in it. For this, engraving on metal was more suitable. Well-known artists took to illustrating books, and many of the most famous painters of the Renaissance were also illustrators. In the eighteenth century, wood-engraving – abandoned for two hundred years – was revived by Thomas Bewick, and in the next

Sir John Tenniel (1820–1914) **Alice offering plum cake to the Lion and the Unicorn**. *Tenniel's imaginative interpretation of the creatures in* **Alice** *did not please Lewis Carroll. The two exchanged many irritable letters, each clinging obstinately to his own point of view.*

*Aubrey Beardsley (1872–
1898)* **The New Star**, *from*
The Rape of the Lock.

century many great illustrations were produced by
lithography (*see page 17*).

While many painters have also been illustrators,
other artists have been interested solely in illustration. Aubrey Beardsley was such an artist. At the
end of the nineteenth century, young artists were
reacting against the "light and colour" paintings of
the Impressionists. They wanted to see Nature
simplified into clear, bold patterns. Beardsley, who
had studied Japanese prints and the work of
Whistler, took this further than most. He distorted
form in order to achieve heavy, massed shapes, and
contrasted these with fine or dotted lines.

Beardsley himself was an extraordinary young
man. He leapt to fame almost overnight at only

Beatrix Potter (1866–1943)
Mouse from **The Tailor of**
Gloucester. *Tate Gallery,*
London. This was Beatrix
Potter's own favourite among
all her books.

twenty-one, and was almost as exotic in his appearance as in his drawings. Always dressed immaculately in a black cutaway coat and silk hat, he carried lemon-yellow kid gloves and wore his hair plastered down over his forehead in a quiff almost to his eyes. No doubt his "elders and betters" disapproved of him very strongly. Whether he would have grown more sober with age we shall never know, for he died at only twenty-five.

In complete contrast is Sir John Tenniel, famous for his illustrations of Lewis Carroll's *Alice*. Tenniel, who was mainly a political cartoonist, drew his last page for the magazine *Punch* sixty-five years after his first. In interpreting the characters in *Alice in Wonderland* and *Through the Looking Glass*, he was helped by Lewis Carroll's own sketches. But of all the ninety-two drawings Tenniel produced for *Alice*, Carroll liked only one – Humpty Dumpty. By profession a mathematician, Carroll based his criticisms, not on artistic merit, but on how many lines the artist had drawn to the square inch!

Arthur Rackham. The Mad
Hatter's tea-party, from **Alice**
in Wonderland.

A 14th-century French miniature, illustrating a story called The Three Women of Paris.

Edmund Dulac. Scene from a Hans Andersen fairy-tale.

Despite this, Tenniel must have been inspired by Carroll's "nonsense" writing, for his illustrations are as essential a part of *Alice* as the author's words.

Beatrix Potter wrote and illustrated only children's books, and her success was possibly due to her strong and vivid memories of her own childhood. Most of us can remember little that happened to us before the age of about five, and even later memories are often rather muzzy. Beatrix Potter, however, could remember quite clearly from the age of one or two – not only people and places but her own feelings, and the experience of learning to walk. She spent a good deal of her childhood in the Scottish highlands, in the care of a nurse who believed firmly in witches and fairies, and this must have made a strong impression on her. She certainly had an uncanny knowledge of what children liked. All her well-loved books, such as *Jemima Puddle-duck, Mrs. Tiggywinkle* and *The Tailor of Gloucester* started as "story-letters" written to the children with whom she had made friends.

Photographs

THE word camera means "room" and the first camera was, in fact, a room – the *camera obscura* or "dark room". If a sheet of paper were held about a foot away from a lens set in its outer wall, a picture of the outside view would appear. The only trouble was, there was no way of keeping the picture on the paper. Eventually, experiments were made in coating the paper with silver nitrate. A Frenchman tried this in 1816, but afterwards complained that the background was black, and the objects on it white. Had he only known it, he had made the first negative!

By the 1850's portrait photography was becoming popular. Unfortunately, some rascally "photographers" took advantage of this. It seems strange now, but there were many people at that time who had only the vaguest idea of what they looked like. A fake "photographer" would simply select a picture that looked fairly like a particular customer. He would then pretend to take a photograph, and shortly afterwards he would present the customer with his "portrait".

Photography's most startling contribution to art and science lay in the recording of motion. In 1872 the ex-Governor of California bet a friend $25,000 that a horse had all four feet off the ground at some time during a race. A photographer called Eadward Muybridge set out to prove this, and eventually did so by using as many as a hundred cameras. Muybridge's pictures created a sensation when they were published. No one had ever managed to "freeze" motion before. Artists had always painted galloping horses with front legs thrust forwards and rear legs thrust backwards, but now they were proved wrong.

In 1880 Muybridge gave a demonstration at which he projected his pictures on to a screen one after another, very quickly. The horse was seen to gallop, and moving pictures were born!

Eadward Muybridge
Muybridge spent several years perfecting his method of "freezing" movement. Basically, he did it by ranging a battery of cameras along one side of a racetrack, and building a reflector opposite them. Threads, attached to shutters on the cameras, were stretched across the track. As the horse rushed by he broke the threads, so tripping the shutters.

Eadward Muybridge (1830–1904) **Galloping Horse**.

Above: Julia Margaret Cameron (1815–79) **Alfred Lord Tennyson**. *This portrait is sometimes known as the "Dirty Monk".*

Julia Margaret Cameron

Mrs Cameron's portrait photographs, now thought to be among the finest ever taken, were not popular with her fellow-Victorians, who thought these unretouched close-ups too truthful – even ugly. They preferred posed, artificial pictures like those by their favourite painters. Mrs Cameron's "painting" photographs, with titles such as "Pray God, bring Father safely home!" now seem so sentimental as to be merely silly.

Tennyson's poems provided Mrs Cameron with most of her inspiration, and she was always searching for faces to fit the characters in them. Once, attending a party with Tennyson, she met a bishop who seemed to her the ideal knightly figure.

"Alfred, I have found Sir Lancelot!" she cried. Tennyson was short-sighted and could not see whom she meant. Attracting attention with his deep, resonant voice he replied, "I want a face well-worn with evil passion!"

Posters

Henri de Toulouse-Lautrec (1864–1901) Poster announcing the appearance of Jane Avril at the Jardin de Paris. This skinny, red-haired English dancer fascinated Lautrec. Here he shows her kicking her leg high above the audience, her pose framed by the neck of a cello grasped by an unseen member of the orchestra. By this device Lautrec focussed attention on the attractions of both dancer and music at the same time.

PEOPLE seldom have time to linger and examine a poster, or read many of the words on it. The picture alone must be both striking enough to arrest attention, and informative enough to convey its message clearly and quickly. The problems involved in making such a picture have come to be appreciated today, and as a result there is a great deal of popular interest in posters. Old posters are being reprinted, and particularly prized among these are the lithographs of Henri de Toulouse-Lautrec.

Born into an aristocratic family, Toulouse-Lautrec broke both his legs in a childhood accident, so stunting their growth. Happily this did not limit his development as a painter. Fascinated by the life of the Paris music-halls, he painted harshly-realistic portraits of the girls who danced in them. His posters, blending abandoned gaiety with absinthe-drinking squalor, lent Paris a "wicked" allure for the English in the 1890's.

You may well feel that posters, photographs and illustrations do not belong in the same book as paintings by great artists of the past. We must remember, however, that they are all pictures, and pictures are what we set out to look at. Even the famous painters of the Renaissance had to work under orders from their patrons, and produce the kind of pictures they were asked for. Today many artists work in the same way for commerce, but this does not mean that their pictures are not worth looking at.

Whenever we look at any picture, however it was made, we should consider three important things. Why did the artist want to make it in the first place? Why did he treat it in the way that he did? And what did people in his own time think about it? If we think of each picture as a whole, in this way, we will understand it much better. We will also find much greater enjoyment in looking at it.

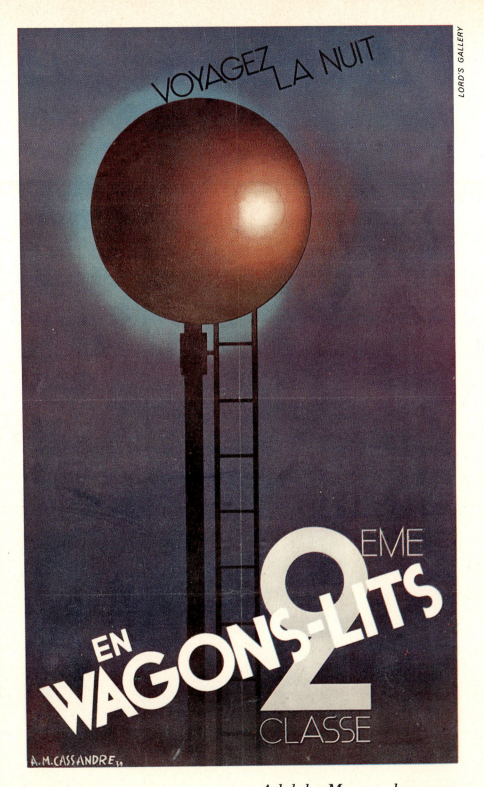

Adolphe Mouron, known as Cassandre (1901–1969) Railway poster. Today's travel advertisements generally stress the comfort of the journey, or the beauty of the scenery. Cassandre's great posters of the 1930's simply made the spine tingle with the sheer adventure of boarding a great liner, or hurtling through the night along gleaming rails of steel.

Acknowledgements

All paintings in the National Gallery are reproduced by courtesy of the Trustees, the National Gallery, London. "A Married Couple" by George Grosz is reproduced by kind permission of the Estate of George Grosz, Princeton, New Jersey. The drawing by Beatrix Potter from *The Tailor of Gloucester* is reproduced by kind permission of Frederick Warne and Company Limited, publishers of *The Tailor of Gloucester*.

Index

*Words and figures in italic refer to
illustrations.*